C.A.R.E.

Life Lessons from the Parables of Jesus

Gerald Briscoe

Table of Contents

Dedication 4

Acknowledgment 5

Chapter 1 Abundant iLife.....................................6

Chapter 2 The Parables of Jesus..........................15

Chapter 3 The Other Parables of Jesus.............. 31

Epilogue... 79

About the Author 80

Dedication

One of the most significant challenges we face in life is keeping an open mind. If we assume we already have all the answers, we will keep ourselves from being open to new information that could help us grow. It seems especially true in the Christian community. So, I want to dedicate this to all those who are willing to read the scriptures with an open mind and look for the life lessons they contain, and find ways to apply those lessons to their own lives, especially in the life and teachings of Jesus.

Acknowledgment

When we started our Zoom Bible study during the pandemic, several people stuck with me for almost 5 years. It was their input, especially when going through the parables of Jesus, that helped write this book. It was their encouragement that helped me keep on going. So, thank you.

Chapter 1
Abundant Life

In writing this book, I remembered what Jesus said about why He came: *"I came so you could have life and have it more abundantly."*

So, what does an abundant life look like? How do you describe it? And is it the same for all of us? Let me share a few of my thoughts, and keep in mind that these are *my* thoughts; they don't represent the whole picture.

When we were on the island of Maui with our family, I took this picture. It's a good visual representation of what an abundant life means to me.

If you notice the tree in the center of the picture, it symbolizes life itself in many religions. Behind the tree, you can see mountains. We all have our mountains to climb. Sometimes we complain about them and wish we didn't have to climb them at all. However, the truth is that those mountains make us stronger and shape who we are. We learn and grow because of our struggles.

Notice the dark clouds. We all go through stormy times of difficulty and challenge. That's just part of life. What matters is how we respond or react to those challenges. I read somewhere that there are only two kinds of people: those who say, *"If only I hadn't said that or done that,"* and those who say, *"What can I learn from this? How could I have done it better or said it differently?"* There's no future in "if only." *Next time* has a future.

But did you notice in the picture that the sun came out again? Dr. Norman Vincent Peale had a picture of a long boat washed up on the shore behind his desk. Under it were the words: *"This too shall pass."* The tide will come back in. There are also blue-sky days, and we need those days to recuperate.

If we examine any one of these pieces of the picture by itself, it's not particularly impressive. But when we look at all the pieces together, it makes a great picture. That's the way life is: taken all together, it makes for a rich and abundant life.

Most articles I've read, and most people I've talked with, say we are not here by accident. We are here for a purpose. God has allowed us to be part of His master plan. If this is true, and I believe it is, we should feel proud of ourselves for realizing that God trusts us enough to include us in His master plan. God would never set us up for failure, so He must have given us the tools and talents to accomplish our purpose.

Mark Twain said that the two most important dates in anyone's life are the day we are born and the day we find out why.

Our journey is to discover our unique purpose and talents. It's about nurturing our abilities and being prepared to use them to serve God by helping others. Knowing our unique purpose, developing our skills, and using them to help others is undeniably a significant part of what it means to live an abundant life.

But how do we go about doing that? It takes work. It takes time, lots of effort, and sacrifice. How do we prepare ourselves to be used by God and be the best "us" we can be?

We could use several models to become the best "us" we can be, but this is the one that appeals to me the most. It may help you, too. It's called **"CARE."** Here's what the acronym represents for me:

C–Christ-centered: Centering our lives around the life and teachings of Jesus.

A–Accepting: Accepting others as they are and where they are in their walk through life, and allowing them to grow at their own pace and in their own way.

R–Responsive: Responding to the needs of others and providing an atmosphere that allows growth.

E–Encourager: Looking for the good in people and encouraging them to be their best. No one grows in an atmosphere of criticism.

Christ-centered

If we want to show others we care about them, we must start by caring about ourselves. You can't give away what you don't have. If we want to help others become Christ-centered, we must first become Christ-centered ourselves.

We have to center our lives around the life and teachings of Jesus. The only records of Jesus' life and teachings are found in the New Testament, so that's where we must start. But don't just study the

Scriptures; think and pray about what you read. Ask God to help you understand how to apply it to your life today. Another option is to study the lives of individuals who have dedicated themselves to living that way.

Ask yourself: *Do I want the results they seem to have accomplished in their lives, in my life? Is it possible for me to live like that?* It may seem like an impossible goal, but believe me, it is not.

A few years ago, I attended a seminar where the speaker provided us with a list of Jesus' attributes. There were around forty in total. He asked us to put an "A" beside each one that related to our attitude and an "L" beside those that had to be learned. We found that almost all of the attributes were related to attitude. Very few had to be learned.

The good news is that we can control our attitudes, so most of Jesus' attributes can be ours simply by changing our perspective. It's still not easy and takes a lifetime to work on, but we can gradually improve.

In our minister's sermons and our Sunday School discussions, we talk about being witnesses for Christ. Whether we like it or not, we are Jesus' representatives on earth. We are the only example that most non-Christians have of Him; it's what they see in our lives. That's a little scary to think about.

Zig Zeigler once said, *"People don't care how much we know until they know how much we care."* People won't be attracted to us or to our church if they feel we don't care about them. They're looking for meaningful relationships with others and with God. If we center our lives around the life and teachings of Jesus, others will be able to tell.

Building a solid foundation: Matt: 7:24–27, Luke 6:46–49.

Centering our lives around the life and teachings of Jesus is that solid foundation.

Another aspect of a strong foundation is maintaining a balanced approach in all the significant areas of life: business (work), home, social, mental, physical, and spiritual. These six areas are so interrelated that they can't be separated. When any of these areas is out of balance, the others are affected as well. The proper balance is different for each of us, depending on our purpose and the stage of life we are in.

Accepting

We accept other people as they are and where they are in their walk-through life. We don't all come to the table with the same background, abilities, or level of understanding.

My knowledge is not perfect. I make a lot of mistakes, and my relationship with Jesus is not what I want it to be. But based on what the Scriptures tell me, Jesus accepts me just as I am anyway, and He expects me to accept others just as they are, too. But that's not easy to do.

In order to accept others as they are and where they are, you have to start by accepting yourself. How well do you accept yourself? Skip Ross, one of my mentors in life, says that you will never go beyond the picture you have of yourself, your self-image. How you feel about that picture is your self-esteem. It's hard to love and accept others if you don't love and accept yourself.

So here are some questions to think about:

- What Scriptures or evidence do we have that Jesus accepts people unconditionally?

- How do you feel about yourself? Do you accept yourself as you are?
- How does it make you feel to know that you are totally accepted by Jesus just as you are?
- Are there people in your life that you have a hard time accepting?
- How do you handle it?

When Judy and I were still in Ottawa, KS, we had a Sunday School teacher who talked about this. She suggested that if there was someone, we were having trouble accepting, we should pray for them and start looking for things we liked about them. I tried this with someone I was having a problem with, and after about two weeks, I had a totally different opinion about them.

We usually find what we look for, so practice looking for the good in others, and you'll find it. And if you can, find ways to let them know what you see. It may change your attitude about them, and theirs about you. You may even find that you like them.

We are encouraged to look for the good in others and let them know what we find. Like I said, no one grows in an atmosphere of criticism. We all want to feel that our lives matter.

Responsive

We are responsive to others' needs, striving to provide an atmosphere where we can all grow personally and discover our unique God-given talents and abilities. We are encouraged to develop our talents to the fullest and are given opportunities to use them in God's service.

People are different and have diverse needs. How can we inclusively address those needs in a way that shows them that we genuinely care? What are some of the basic needs we all have? What are people looking for?

Psychologists tell us that one of our basic needs is to feel that our lives matter and that we have value. We are not accidents. We're here for a purpose and have the talents and abilities to accomplish that purpose. One way we can help people realize their value is by helping them discover their purpose, develop their talents, and provide them with opportunities to use those talents to serve God.

Jesus said He came so we could have life and have it more abundantly. Knowing your purpose and having the opportunity to be part of God's plan would undoubtedly qualify as part of an abundant life.

Another basic need we all have is meaningful relationships with others and God. We can foster connections by allowing people to participate in Bible studies, Sunday School classes, or groups that focus on personal growth.

One thing I keep repeating is that no one grows in an atmosphere of criticism. Most of the time, we don't need to be told what we did wrong; we already know. Start by letting people know what they did right. Practice looking for the good in people and telling them what you find before making any constructive suggestions. Many times, even constructive suggestions are not as helpful as simply telling someone what they did right.

What could you add to this to help you respond to people's needs? Do you have talents you would like to use to respond to other people's needs? How can we provide the environment for you to develop and use those talents?

We always find what we focus our attention on. If we look for the negative characteristics in people, that's what we'll see. If we look for the good, that's what we'll find.

We all have God-Given talents, but many of us don't believe in ourselves enough to recognize them or believe we are worthy of developing them. We think it's possible for others but not for us. Sometimes we just need someone to give us a word of encouragement.

In her book *Silver Boxes*, Florence Littauer tells the story of her dad, who wanted to be a writer. He even wrote articles and submitted them to a local newspaper or to his church newsletter, and several of them were accepted. However, his wife told him that he wasn't good enough to be a writer, so he never pursued it. What would have happened if she had given him some encouragement instead?

Skip Ross, in his *Dynamic Living Seminars*, challenges us to look only for the good in people, especially those we have a problem with, and only talk about the good, verbally or in our self-talk, for 90 days. If you fail for even one day, you must start over. He says it will change your life for the better.

What would happen if we looked for the good in people and let them know the good we found? Everyone wants to feel that their lives matter. Psychologists tell us that recognition is something that babies cry for and grown men and women die for. Could this be part of what it means to live by the Golden Rule?

Encourage

I thought of several words, like *edifying, empowering,* and *enthusiasm,* but the word *"encourage"* seems to fit best. I feel that God is calling us to be encouragers, especially now.

C.A.R.E.

I have given over 20 copies of my first book, *Lessons from the Back of the Store,* to people whose opinions I respected. I was hoping to receive some positive suggestions. When I didn't receive any replies, I assumed they either didn't read it or didn't like it. I was getting a little disappointed. Then, I finally received some responses. The comments I received were encouraging, and they encouraged me to keep on writing. It's amazing what even one encouraging comment can do for you.

Chapter 2
The Parables of Jesus

What is a parable, and why did Jesus use parables to teach His moral principles?

A parable is a short and simple story that illustrates a moral attitude or religious principle. There are at least 43 parables that Jesus used to teach the lessons He wanted to share. He was a master at finding illusions in their culture and in everyday life to convey his moral principles. Psychologists tell us that while we may forget the moral lesson, we will remember the story used to teach it, and through it, remember the lesson taught.

In my first book, *Lessons from the Back of the Store*, I talked about 13 principles I wanted to pass on to my children and grandchildren. I used stories from my childhood to illustrate them. From the responses I have gotten from people, it was clear that it was the stories people remembered and enjoyed the most.

The Kingdom of God

The Kingdom of God was one of Jesus' favorite topics. There are at least 13 parables devoted to describing it. Each one of them gives us an example or description of what the Kingdom of God is like and how we can become part of it.

The Parable of the Hidden Treasure

Matthew 13:44 – *"So he replied, 'This means, then, that every teacher of the Law who becomes a disciple in the Kingdom of Heaven is like the owner of a house who takes new and old things out of his storeroom.'"*

My dad obtained his pharmacy license after completing nine years of correspondence courses while working full-time and raising three kids, all during the Depression. I earned my pharmacy degree after four and a half years of college. Today, when pharmacists obtain their license, they are considered doctors of pharmacy. Each advance was made possible by the previous generation. We didn't discard their knowledge; we built upon it.

The Pharisees and scribes spent all their time studying the Scriptures. They felt they knew all there was to know and closed their minds to anything new. However, for those who did open their minds to the possibility of something new and listened to what Jesus had to say, they became disciples of the Kingdom of God.

Jesus is saying that they didn't have to discard all of the knowledge they already had; instead, they could apply this new knowledge to enhance their existing understanding. It made the old knowledge understandable.

The lesson for us is to be open to learning new things. If you feel you already know everything you need to know, there is no opportunity to grow and become more of what God wants us to be. He has more in store for us, but we must be open to receiving it.

I don't believe for a moment that God orchestrated this pandemic, but I do believe that He can utilize the circumstances it created to steer us closer to His ultimate will of establishing the Kingdom of God on earth.

What signs can you discern that this is true?

What actions can we take to ensure that this is indeed the case?

The Parable of the Pearl of Great Price

Matthew 13:45-46 – *"Also, the Kingdom of Heaven is like this: A man is looking for fine pearls, and when he finds one that is unusually fine, he goes and sells everything he has, and buys that pearl."*

The message here is similar to that of the hidden treasure, but with a difference. William Barclay says, *"The man who was digging in the field was not searching for treasure; it came on him all unaware. The man who was searching for pearls was spending his life in the search. But no matter whether the discovery was the result of a moment or the result of a lifetime's search, the reaction was the same—everything had to be sold and sacrificed to gain the precious thing. Once again, we are left with the same truth—that, however a man discovers the will of God for himself, whether it be in the lightning flash of a moment's illumination or at the end of a long and conscious search, it is worth anything unhesitatingly to accept it."*

The Parable of the Net

Matthew 13:46-50 – "The Kingdom of God is like a net that was let down into the lake and caught all kinds of fish. When it was full, the fishermen pulled it up on the shore. Then they sat down and collected the good fish in baskets, but threw the bad away. This is how it will be at the end of the age. The angels will come and separate the wicked from the righteous and throw them into the fiery furnace, where there will be weeping and gnashing of teeth."

The nature of the dragnet is that it does not discriminate. It catches everything, the good and the bad. The only fish they considered good were ones with scales. The rest were thrown back into the sea or disposed of.

Our lesson here is that it's not our responsibility to judge. We only know part of the story of other people's lives. Only God knows the whole story. We are responsible for accepting people as they are and where they are in their spiritual journey, and letting them grow. The separation is God's. Our role is to be the best example of what it means to be part of the Kingdom of God on earth. Hopefully, others will see something in us that they want for themselves.

Jesus couldn't make people choose to be the good, productive soil; He could only sow the seed.

A quote from Dr. John Maxwell resonated with me: *"People buy into the leader before they buy into the vision. People buy into the vision after the leader buys into it."*

What's your vision of the Kingdom of God?

Have you bought into that vision, and can other people see that you've bought into it based on how you live your life?

I don't know about you, but I still have a long way to go. I'm still growing.

The Parable of the Mustard Seed

Mark 4:30-32; Matthew 13:31-32; Luke 13:18-19 – *"Again He said, 'What shall we say the Kingdom of God is like, or what parable shall we use to describe it? It is like a mustard seed, which is the smallest seed you plant in the ground. Yet when planted, it grows and becomes the largest of all garden plants, with such big branches that the birds of the air can perch in its shade.'"*

Whenever Jews spoke of something small, they used the mustard seed as an example. Most mustard plants were only about five feet tall, but they could grow up to be as tall as twelve feet. It wasn't uncommon to see these trees full of birds, because they loved the little black seeds.

The whole point of the parable is that the Kingdom of God starts small, but no one knows where it will end. Empires were often pictured as great trees with subject nations depicted as birds finding shelter within their branches. Jesus is saying that this is the way it is with the Kingdom of God. It will start small, but will eventually include many nations. It also means that the Kingdom of God is big enough to take in people of many different faiths, beliefs, and nationalities that exist.

An idea that can change the world starts with one person. When it takes hold of someone, it can be unstoppable. Look at what happened with Facebook, Amazon, or Zoom. They may or may not be good, depending on your point of view, but they do represent what can happen when an idea catches on. Maybe some good ideas will come out of this pandemic that will catch on and change the world for the better. Likewise, Jesus started with twelve disciples, and today, there are approximately over two billion Christians worldwide, with likely some in every country.

In William Barclay's commentary, he shares a story from one of Cecil Northcott's books about a group of young people from many nations discussing how the Christian gospel could be spread. They talked of propaganda, of literature, of all the ways of disseminating the gospel in the twentieth century.

Then the girl from Africa spoke, "When we want to take Christianity to one of our villages," she said, "we don't send them books. We take a Christian family and send them to live in the village, and they make the village Christian by living there."

It can start with one person becoming a living example of what it means to be a Christian. The parable tells us that we are the example of what it means to live a Christian life. We have to be the small beginning – the mustard seed – that will grow into the Kingdom of God on earth.

The Parable of the Yeast

Matthew 13:33 – "The Kingdom of Heaven is like yeast that a woman took and mixed into a large amount of flour until it worked all through the dough."

It's fascinating that Jesus used yeast to illustrate the Kingdom of God. The Jews looked at yeast as a symbol of corruption or putrefaction. The point of this parable is the same as it was with the mustard seed: the Kingdom of God will start small but eventually become very large.

The small piece of leaven left over from a previous baking would eventually permeate the whole batch of flour. Jesus said it was "three measures of flour," so I had to look it up to see how much that was. It turns out that's enough flour, according to an article I found on *The Bread Monk* (2012), to make 52 loaves of bread, each weighing about one and a half pounds. If you got 16 slices out of a loaf, that's enough to make 416 peanut butter and jelly sandwiches. Can you picture a woman kneading that much dough? Jesus sometimes used exaggerated illustrations to get His listeners' attention so they would listen to what He had to say.

Another thing Jesus said in this parable that would have gotten their attention, besides using yeast and an enormous amount of flour, was that He used a woman. Women were not highly thought of in Jesus' day. They were better off than in some cultures, but still second-rate citizens. Jesus treated women with respect and compassion. In this parable, He depicts a woman as an agent of the Kingdom. The parable's message is that the Kingdom of Heaven is like a woman who wants to do more than feed her family. She wants to feed the entire village, and possibly the whole world. In other words, the Kingdom is for everybody.

What's the message for us today? The same as the mustard seed. We have to be the small lump of leaven that will help permeate all the flour. We have to be that lump of leaven right where we are, in our area of influence.

The Parable of the Great Banquet

Scripture: Luke 14:1-24

The parable, found in verses 15-24, helps us understand what's going on and why Jesus gave this parable if you read from verse one. There are many life lessons to be learned from this. It says that Jesus was having a meal with a prominent Pharisee. The religious leaders watched His every move, trying to catch Him doing something violating their laws, such as healing on the Sabbath. How many people watch us to see if our words and actions match up? Do our words have any meaning if they don't match our actions?

Another significant lesson from the Parable of the Great Banquet is the value of humility. It teaches us that it's better to accept a lower position and be asked to move up than to accept a higher position and be asked to move down. This principle of humility is a powerful reminder to be modest in our achievements and to let others acknowledge our worth. It can guide us in our interactions with others and our pursuit of a humble and righteous life.

Then there was the Pharisee at the meal who suggested that the man who would eat at the feast in the Kingdom of God was blessed. This statement is what prompted Jesus to tell this parable. What was the concept of this feast in the Kingdom of God? Who was going to be there?

Their idea was that it would be only Jews, and no sinners, Samaritans, or Gentiles. It was going to be a pretty exclusive banquet. Who are we excluding from God's table with our actions and attitudes, intentionally or unintentionally? Sometimes, what we say, verbally or with our body language, suggests to people that they don't belong. But Jesus says that God's table is big enough for everyone who wants to come.

Many were invited, but some made excuses for not coming. Were their excuses valid? Who buys land sight unseen? Who buys a team of oxen before trying them out first? How often do we make excuses for not doing something we don't want to do? How often have we felt God nudging us to do something without following through on it?

Have you ever allowed family activities to crowd out commitments to God? There's time for everything. They say you can tell a lot about where a person's heart is by looking at their cheque book, where they spend their money, or their planner, where they spend their time, and also by examining their excuses. I don't know about you, but I still have much growing to do.

The Parable of the Ten Virgins

Matthew 25:1-13 – *"At that time, the Kingdom of Heaven will be like this. Once there were ten young women who took their oil lamps and went out to meet the bridegroom. Five of them were foolish, and the other five were wise. The foolish ones took their lamps but did not take any extra oil with them, while the wise ones took containers full of oil for their lamps.*

The bridegroom was late in coming, so the women began to

nod and fall asleep. It was already midnight when the cry rang out, 'Here is the bridegroom! Come and meet him!' The ten women woke up and trimmed their lamps. Then the foolish ones said to the wise ones, 'Let us have some of your oil because our lamps are going out.'

'No, indeed,' the wise ones answered, 'there is not enough for you and for us. Go to the shop and buy some for yourselves.' So the foolish women went off to buy some oil, and while they were gone, the bridegroom arrived. The five who were ready went in with him to the wedding feast, and the door was closed.

Later, the other women arrived. 'Sir, sir! Let us in!' they cried out. 'Certainly not! I don't know you,' the bridegroom answered.

And Jesus concluded, 'Be on your guard, then, because you do not know the day or the hour.'"

This story of the ten virgins illustrates the importance of preparing ourselves to be used by God. We never know when opportunities will come our way or when our time on earth will come to an end.

When the opportunities come, we want to have our "lamps trimmed and with plenty of oil," so we can be ready to be used by God and be the best examples of Jesus for others. The lesson here is that we never know when those opportunities will come.

The Parable of the Talents

Scripture: Matthew 25:14-30

This parable was directed toward the Scribes and Pharisees. Their primary aim was to uphold the law exactly as it stood, which led to a paralysis of religious truth. They were supposed to be an example of how to have a meaningful relationship with God, but instead, they used their gifts to build a fence around the law that kept other people out. They buried their talent in the ground.

In case you're wondering, a *talent* was not a coin but a measure, probably made of silver. A talent of silver was worth about $240, so five talents were worth about $ 1,200. That was equal to about twenty years of income for a day laborer. In today's value, a talent would be worth about $400,000, or $2,000,000 for five talents. But the size of the talent wasn't the point of the parable.

This parable offers several good life lessons, but I want to share three main ones with you.

Verse 15 says they were given talents, each according to their ability. God will not give us responsibilities beyond what we can handle. What mattered was not the size of the talent but that we used what we had.

In this parable, the one with five talents and the one with two talents doubled what they were given. What was the result? They were trusted with more responsibility. The more we use our gifts, the better we get, and the more opportunities will open up for us.

It's also true that if we don't use our gifts, they diminish. You lose what you don't use or stop using. So, why didn't the man in the parable use the gift he had been given? Why don't we use the talents we've been given? There could be several reasons. Here are a few.

1. Fear of failure. No one does anything perfectly the first time. Failure is our teacher. It's only a failure if you don't learn from it and keep on trying.

2. Fear of punishment. He lost his talent because he didn't try.

3. Fear of the responsibility of success.

4. Not believing in ourselves. If we don't believe we are worthy of success or worthy of being loved by God, we may not even try.

God has given us all a purpose and abundant talents to accomplish that purpose. The size of our purpose or the amount of our talents doesn't matter. The only thing that matters is that we try. If we try, then God will be there to guide and help us.

The Parable of the Unmerciful Servant

Scripture: Matthew 18:23-24

Almost all parables have a central point, and this one is about the need to forgive others in order to be part of the Kingdom of God. If God has forgiven us for our wrongdoings, then we need to forgive others for theirs, especially for what they've done to us or against us.

If Jesus can pray from the cross and ask God to forgive those who are doing to him what they are doing, shouldn't we follow His example? But what does it mean to forgive? How many times do we forgive someone? What should our relationship with the ones we forgive look like in the future? Does that relationship go back to the way it was? I certainly don't have all the answers, but here are my thoughts.

First, Peter asked Jesus how many times we should forgive, and then answered his question. He suggested seven times. Based on the Old Testament thought, you forgive three times, but not the fourth time.

Peter thought he was generous by suggesting seven times, but Jesus answered, not seven times, but seventy times seven. In other words, there are no limits on how many times we should forgive.

What if someone comes to you and asks for forgiveness for

something they did or said that harmed or offended you somehow, and just by the tone of their voice or other nonverbal communications, you knew they weren't sincere? What do you do then? You can forgive them, but can your relationship return to how it was?

Our son-in-law, Dave, worked as an administrative pastor in a large church. The head pastor hired one of his friends to take over some of his duties and then fired Dave. A year later, the pastor asked Dave to have lunch with him and admitted he had made a mistake. He asked Dave to forgive him and return to work with him again. Dave said, "I can forgive you, but I can't come back to work for you because I can't trust you." Once trust in someone is lost, how can it be restored? When you forgive someone, who benefits the most, the person you forgive or you?

Here's another thought: what if they aren't even aware that what they said or did was offensive or hurtful? What if it's just our perception that it was wrong? Sometimes, we rehearse that perceived wrong repeatedly in our minds until it takes on a life of its own. Will this affect our relationship with that person? What if, instead, we went to them and asked them about it? Most perceived wrongs would disappear, and the relationships would be saved.

If God is the kind of God Jesus says He is, we need to learn to forgive others to have the type of relationship we want with Him. An unforgiving spirit seems to me to be incompatible with the forgiving spirit of God.

Forgiveness is an area in which I still need to grow a lot. I've never been in a situation that requires me to forgive someone for something significant, and I don't know whether I would be up for the challenge. I hope I will, but I also hope that I never have to find out.

The Parable of the Growing Seed

Mark 4:26-29 – "Jesus went on to say, 'The Kingdom of God is like this. A man scatters seed in his field. He sleeps at night and is up and about during the day, and all the while the seeds are sprouting and growing. Yet he does not know how it happens. The soil itself makes the plants grow and bear fruit; first, the tender stalk appears, then the ear, and finally the ear full of corn. When the corn is ripe, the man starts cutting it with his sickle, because harvest time has come.'"

This parable is only found in Mark. It's followed by the parable of the mustard seed and includes some valuable lessons for us. It says that the Kingdom of God is growing all the time, even though that growth is not visible on a day-by-day basis. It's going to grow in spite of us.

That does not mean we can sit by and allow it to grow while doing nothing. So what is our responsibility? A farmer doesn't just plant the seed and then do nothing. He waters it and provides fertilizer so the seed can reach its full potential.

By discovering our purpose, developing our talents, and allowing God to use us, we become the water and the fertilizer that allow the Kingdom of God to grow. We can't always see it grow. Like the plant, growth is only seen over time. We don't know how it's growing, but it is.

One lesson for us is to have patience. Our responsibility is to be the water and fertilizer (the example of our lives) and allow God to do the rest.

Another lesson for us is to be prepared. We don't know when the harvest time is, but it will come.

The Parable of the Workers in the Vineyard

Scripture: Matthew 20:1-16

It helps us understand this parable if we are familiar with the traditions of that time. The parable describes a common occurrence that frequently happened in Palestine, especially during certain periods.

The grape harvest occurred at the end of September, followed by the rains. If the harvest wasn't completed before the rains came, it could be ruined. So any worker was welcome, even if they could only work for an hour. The wage for a day's work was a *denarius* (about four cents), roughly the amount it would take to feed a family for a day.

The workers would stand in the marketplace waiting to be hired. Some of them stood there until 5 p.m., hoping for work. These men were the lowest class of workers. They weren't attached to any group. If they were not hired, even for one day, it could be a disaster for them financially. The day ended for them at 6 p.m., so 5 p.m. was the last hour of the workday.

Here are some observations about the lessons for us, taken from the commentary by William Barclay:

In one sense, it serves as a warning to us, especially if we have become part of the Kingdom of God early in life. Others will come after us, and we can't claim any special privilege over them. Everyone, no matter when they came, is equally precious to God.

This was also a warning to the Jews. They were the chosen people, but they looked down on others, like the Gentiles. Their attitude toward the Gentiles was that "the only good Gentile was a dead Gentile." This attitude was sometimes carried over into the Christian church.

In this parable, we also see the comfort of God. No matter when we come into the Kingdom of God, early in life or late in life, or no matter what we accomplish, we are equally welcomed.

Here we see the compassion of God. Someone may have skills and may have even developed them, but hasn't found a way to use them. No one has "hired" them until the last hour. But in God's economy, they get the same wages as those who worked all day.

It illustrates the generosity of God. They didn't all do the same amount of work, but they all received the same pay. All service for God ranks the same with Him. It's not the amount, but the spirit in which it is done, that matters.

All God gives us is grace. We can't earn a reward or a favored place from Him. The whole point of our work is the spirit in which it is done. Are we Christians because of the reward we expect, or because of the joy of serving God and other people?

The Lord's Prayer

Here's one last thought about the Kingdom of God. This is not a parable, but it gives us the clearest picture of what Jesus meant by "The Kingdom of God."

Jewish writers had an interesting writing style: they would say something in one sentence, then clarify what they meant in the next sentence. This is what happens in the Lord's prayer.

In the first sentence, *"Thy Kingdom Come"* is followed by *"Thy will be done on earth as it is in heaven."* So, the Kingdom of God will come when we live by God's will here on earth as perfectly as it is done in heaven.

I don't know if I have ever measured up to that description, but I am growing in that direction. That's the goal we all should strive for.

Chapter 3
The Other Parables of Jesus

Jesus taught about many other things besides the Kingdom of Heaven. He was a master at using examples from everyday life and from their culture to teach the life lessons and principles He wanted to share.

Let's go through the other parables Jesus taught to see the life lessons He gave and how we can apply those lessons to our lives today.

The Parable of the Sower

Matthew 13:1-23; Mark 4:3-25; Luke 8:5-15

Jesus was a master at taking what was happening at the moment and using it to teach the lesson He wanted to share with His audience. William Barclay says that Jesus was preaching from a boat on the shore and looked up and saw someone sowing seed in a field on the hillside.

It helps to understand what the fields looked like in Jesus' day. There were pathways in the fields called "waysides," where people could go through the field. Because of that, the soil was packed solid, and the seed sprouting was impossible, so the birds had a meal.

In some places, the soil was very shallow. Just a few inches below, there was sandstone. The sun would warm the sandstone and cause the seed to sprout too soon, before it had time to produce roots deep enough to get the nourishment it needed to sustain itself.

It was impossible to remove all the thistles and roots from the soil. The weeds grew faster than the seed and choked it out. Then there was also the deep, rich soil where the seed could take root and produce a good harvest.

Let's look at these different types of soil and see what we can learn about what Jesus is saying to the people of His day, and what He's saying to us today.

The Hard Soil

Mark 4:3-4 – "A farmer went out to sow his seed. As he was scattering the seed, some fell along the path, and the birds came and ate it up."

This parable is one of my favorites. It remains just as meaningful today as it was in Jesus' time. I see two main lessons in it for us today.

The first lesson is that not everyone will listen to what you have to share, regardless of how great it is or how excited you are. That's just the way it is. Some will "gloss over" and not even hear you. I understand that. I've experienced that too. I've seen the blank looks on faces when I've tried to share something I'm excited about. On occasion, I've given those blank looks myself. I wonder how many great things I missed because I wouldn't listen.

Jesus' responsibility was to "sow the seed." Our responsibility is to decide what we will do with it and what kind of soil we will become.

The second lesson is that it doesn't do any good to chase after people and convince them to change their minds or accept what we have to say. You will waste the time and energy you could use to find someone else who is interested. This lesson has been a hard one for me to learn. When I see that something will be valuable to others, I want them to see it too. But the truth is that nothing we do or say will change their minds if they don't want to.

Just like Jesus, our responsibility is to "sow the seed." Jesus shared God's message with us. It's our responsibility to decide what we will do with it and what kind of soil we will be.

The Rocky Soil

Luke 8:6 – "Other seed fell on rocky ground, where it grew up and withered because there was no moisture."

A famous evangelist once said, "It takes about 5% effort to win someone to Christ and 95% effort to keep them in Christ and growing into maturity in the church."

The rocky ground didn't mean it was filled with rocks. There were areas with only a thin layer of soil, and underneath was a layer of limestone. When the sun came out, it warmed the soil, and the seed sprouted quickly, but there wasn't enough nourishment or water to sustain it, and it withered and died.

William Barclay said there are two reasons people don't stay committed. First, they should have thought it through when they became a Christian, to realize what it means and what it costs before starting. The second is that they never let it get beyond the surface of their lives.

I've known people like that. They get all excited about something, then at the first sign of conflict or challenge, they don't continue. They lack a genuine depth of commitment. They must realize that there will be challenges no matter what they decide. Those challenges will either break you or make you stronger.

I don't want to be just a "surface Christian." But here's a question: How do we commit to Christ without getting out of balance in the other significant areas of life? Or are all the major areas of life so interrelated that we can't separate them?

It seems to me that Christianity is a way of life. It means centering our lives around the life and teachings of Jesus in everything we do.

That's not easy. We need to keep reading the Scriptures, praying, and meditating on their meaning and how to apply what we learn to our daily lives. We need the fellowship of other Christians, especially those who are further along the path to spiritual maturity than we are. We all need mentors in our lives. It's impossible to become mature Christians on our own or in isolation.

The Thorny Soil

Matthew 13:7 – "Other seed fell among thorns, which grew up and choked the plants."

Palestinian farmers were sometimes lazy. They may cut off the tops of weeds and even burn off the tops. The field looked clean, but the weeds' roots were still below the surface. They grew faster than the seed and finally choked out the good seed.

Sometimes things happen that cause us to become sidetracked, and we don't reach our potential or fulfill God's purpose for our lives.

So what are some of the "weeds" that grow along with the "seeds" planted in us? Here are a few:

Fears. Sometimes we doubt our ability to do what we are supposed to do. *If we fail, what will people think? If I'm successful, what about the responsibility that comes with it? Will I be able to* *handle it?*

We worry about the economy. *Will I have enough to provide for my family and still have enough to last through retirement? What if I get sick? What if I get COVID-19?*

So, how do you handle fears? Here are some suggestions:

- **Action.** Do the thing you fear. Most of the time, the fear will go away.

- **Dilution.** Expose yourself to positive things, and be careful what you watch, read, and who you associate with. Use positive affirmations and Bible verses that deal with handling fear.

- **Learn how to love.** Perfect love casts out fear.

Pursuit of riches (wealth). There's nothing wrong with having money. The danger is becoming too comfortable, stopping personal growth, or not using our wealth to serve others or worthy causes.

Pursuit of pleasure. There's nothing wrong with enjoying life and having fun. But sometimes it can get in the way of doing what God wants us to do. It's easy to get out of balance in this area. Growing as a person and doing what we feel God wants from us is not always easy or fun.

Settling for second best. William Barclay says that the worst enemy of the best is the second best. There are many great causes and things to pursue that command our attention. We can get so involved in many things and spread ourselves so thin that we can't do our best in anything.

Work in the other regions. Discover your purpose and talents, and stay in those areas. Let someone else handle what isn't yours to do.

These are just a few "weeds" that can keep us from being all God intends us to be. What are your thoughts?

The Good Soil

Matthew 13:8 – "Still other seed fell on good soil where it produced a crop–some a hundred, sixty, or thirty times what was sown."

So far, we've talked about three types of soil that Jesus mentioned:

- **Hard soil:** Those unreceptive people who close their minds, glaze over, and nothing gets in.

- **Rocky soil:** Those who make a surface commitment and often fail to continue when faced with the first sign of resistance or a negative response.

- **Thorny soil:** Those who get involved in too many things and become ineffective in everything.

Now, let's talk about good soil and how we can prepare the "soil" of our lives so the "seeds" we receive will grow and produce a crop. Here are a few thoughts:

- **Be open-minded.** At least listen to what others say. Maybe God is using them to give you some "seeds" of wisdom.

- **Develop a personal relationship with God.** Talk to God through prayer, then listen for the answers through meditation and God's guidance.

- **Act on what you feel is God's will for you.** Don't wait until you have all the answers before you start. Remember, "God can't steer a parked car." We have to be in motion. Be willing to make mistakes and then make corrections as you go.

- **Keep yourself balanced** in all the significant areas of life: business/work, home, social, physical, financial, mental, and spiritual. When we get out of balance in any area for too long, it affects all the others. They are all interrelated.

- **Find your purpose in life and your areas of giftedness.** Develop your gifts and find ways to use them to serve others. Jesus said that He came so we could have life and have it more abundantly. That's how we have that "abundant life." We must develop our gifts now to be ready when the opportunity arises to serve.

Did you notice that Jesus didn't say we all had to be super successful? We must develop and use our gifts to the best of our ability. The same message is in the parable of the talents. The only one He reprimanded was the one who buried his talent and didn't use it.

What example would Jesus use if He were here with us today?

He might discuss a dynamic speaker sharing their pearls of wisdom, only to see them go over the heads of many listeners or get lost in today's busyness and challenges. At the same time, only a few truly understand and apply those pearls to their lives, ultimately producing results.

These are just a few of my thoughts. What can you add? How are you preparing your "soil" to produce a crop for God?

Life Lessons Recap

Hard Soil

Not everyone will listen and accept the seed we sow. If people are uninterested, don't waste time persuading them to change their minds. Instead, spend your time with those who are. Just like Jesus, it is our responsibility to sow the seed.

Rocky Soil

No matter what we decide to do in life, there will be challenges, but they can strengthen us and help us grow if we learn from them. It's a lifetime journey. We need to keep studying and growing through every stage of life.

The Thorny Soil

The ground full of thorns shows me the importance of knowing our purpose and the cost, so that when other ideas come, we can weigh them against what we want to see if they pull us in the wrong direction or help us fulfill our purpose.

It tells us the importance of making sure what we put into our minds through what we read, watch, and who we associate with will not grow into weeds in our lives. We are creatures of habit. Make sure we are developing habits that won't become "weeds" in our lives.

The Good Soil

The lesson is the importance of knowing ourselves—our purpose and talents—and preparing to serve when opportunities arise. It shows us the need to spend time daily in study, preparation, and meditation. Exposing ourselves to positive, uplifting material and avoiding negative people and things is essential. We must avoid wasting our time with uninterested people. People will accept our seeds only if they want to.

Parable of the Lost Sheep

Matthew 18:12-14 – "What do you think? If a man owns a hundred sheep, and one of them wanders away, will he not leave the ninety-nine on the hills and go to look for the one that wanders off? And if he finds it, truly I tell you, he is happier about that one sheep than the ninety-nine that did not wander off. In the same way, your Father in heaven is not willing that any of these little ones should perish."

Jesus told this parable in response to criticism from the scribes and Pharisees for eating with tax collectors and sinners. They called anyone who didn't follow their rules to the letter "people of the land." According to William Barclay, the Pharisees said you are not to have any dealings with them in any way, especially not to eat with them. In the Middle East, to have anyone eat at your table was the same as making them part of your family. So, by eating with them, Jesus made them part of God's family.

The Pharisees' attitude was not that there will be joy in heaven over one who repents, but *"There will be joy in heaven over one sinner who is obliterated before God."* They looked sadistically forward, not to *saving* one sinner but to the *destruction* of the sinner.

Jesus is saying in this parable that God is like the good shepherd. He cares about all of us and wants a personal relationship with us. But we are sometimes like the sheep that wander off. Sheep sometimes get so focused on eating that they wander away from the rest of the flock and the protection the shepherd provides.

Someone once said that we all have a God-shaped void in our hearts. Sometimes I feel like that sheep. I get so focused on the challenges of the day or my wants that I forget to fill that God-shaped void with things that will improve my relationship with God.

We should strive to maintain a proper balance in all areas of our lives. If any area is out of balance for too long, it will also affect all the other areas. However, the spiritual area is the most critical to keep in balance, and also the easiest one to neglect. We need to develop the habit of spending time in prayer, meditation, and reading the scriptures each day. We have to center our lives around the life and teachings of Jesus. These things help us fill that God-shaped void with things that matter and help us build our relationship with God.

Ask, and You Will Receive

Scripture: Luke 11:5-13

The disciples, seeking guidance, asked Jesus to teach them how to pray. In response, He shared the Lord's Prayer and then told a parable about a friend in need of bread. This parable, rich in symbolism, holds profound lessons about prayer. What could these lessons be? How can we apply them to our lives today? To fully grasp the parable's wisdom, we must look at the context of the time and the culture.

Why would a visitor come to your house at midnight? Many people traveled after sundown to avoid the heat, so this may have been common. Hospitality was a deeply valued custom in the Middle East. When offering hospitality, it couldn't be a meager meal—it had to be a full one. And a meal wasn't complete without bread. The man in the parable likely had everything except bread. Since bread couldn't be preserved, families baked only enough for the day. Women often baked bread in an open courtyard, and perhaps this man's wife had noticed that a neighbor had extra bread. Bread was a big deal because it wasn't just food; it was also their eating utensil, as they didn't use forks or spoons like we do today.

Why didn't the neighbor want to get up and give him bread?

Houses usually consisted of one room with a small window. A raised section held a stove that stayed warm through the night, and the entire family slept on mats around it. They often brought the animals inside, too. Imagine someone knocking at midnight; getting up without waking everyone (and the animals) would be nearly impossible. It's easy to understand his hesitation. But the man persisted, and finally, his friend got up and gave him what he needed to fulfill his duty of hospitality.

Remember, a parable is a comparison meant to reveal truth. This one highlights contrast. If we, imperfect as we are, know how to give good gifts to those we love, how much more will God give to us?

So, what lessons can we learn about prayer from this parable?

- **Ask:** If we don't ask, the answer is automatically no, but we must ask for the right reasons. Are we asking only for personal gain, or for something that adds value to others? The man asked for bread so he could show his guest proper hospitality.

- **Seek:** Look for the answers to your prayers.

- **Be proactive:** don't just wait for God to hand things to you. We must move for guidance to come. The man couldn't meet his guest's needs without help. In the same way, we all need others' help at times.

- **Knock:** If what you're seeking is right and purposeful, keep growing and preparing so that when the door opens, you're ready to walk through it. Persist, and don't give up. What if the man had stopped knocking after the first refusal? Sometimes, we're simply not ready yet for what we're asking for.

These are the lessons I take from this parable. What insights do you draw from it? Your perspective might enrich our understanding.

Lamp on a Stand

Matthew 5:14-15; Mark 4:21-22; Luke 8:16; Luke 11:33 – "You are the light of the world. A city on a hill cannot be hidden. Neither do people light a lamp and put it under a bowl. Instead, they put it on its stand, and it gives light to everyone in the house."

This is an example that everyone would be familiar with. The houses in Jesus' time were small one-room dwellings with only one 18-inch window, so the rooms were quite dark. For light, they used lamps filled with oil with a floating wick. Since they didn't have matches, they sometimes kept the lamp lit. People would typically place the lamp on a lampstand. If they didn't have a lampstand, they would use an overturned bushel basket. When leaving the house, they would put the lamp under the bushel basket instead of blowing it out to protect the home.

In John 8:12, Jesus said, "I am the light of the world." In this parable, He says *we* are the light of the world. What does that mean to you, and how does that make you feel? For me, it means we must shine with the reflection of His light in the world, and that's a tremendous responsibility. It means learning about Jesus and His life so we can reflect Him accurately. For many people, the only "Jesus" they will know is the one they see in us.

Just as the light from a lamp is visible to everyone and serves as a guide, the light within us needs to be seen by others. We must be examples of what it means to be a Christian, not just within the church walls but in our everyday lives. We should reflect the light of Christ in everything we do and say. The "light of Christ" must first be in us, because you can't give away what you don't have.

Have you ever faced a situation where someone suggested doing something that didn't feel right? You just *knew* it wasn't the right thing to do? What did you do? Often, others feel the same but are afraid to speak up. If no one says anything, it will likely happen, but if one person voices concern, others may join in and prevent it from happening.

Here's an example from Judy's experience in high school:

"When I was in high school, Joyce, a friend, and I were walking home from a Friday night football game. As we were walking, a car pulled up beside us with boys from school who asked us to go for a ride. When I noticed they were drinking, I told them I would go ahead and walk home. Joyce wanted to go with them, and I told her that was fine, but I would walk. She got angry with me but didn't get in the car. It damaged our relationship for a while. However, in her first year of college, she had a severe nervous breakdown. One night, she called me and asked if I would go to the movies with her, and I said yes. I saw some of our other friends at the film, and they asked why I was with Joyce. They said she had called all of them to go with her, and they refused because they didn't want to be associated with her. After that, we renewed our friendship, and we enjoyed many years of doing things together."

Building a Strong Foundation

Jesus discussed the importance of building a strong foundation in several of His parables.

Wise and Foolish Builders:

Matthew 7:24-27; Luke 6:47-49

This parable seems just as relevant today as it was in Jesus' time. How many of us feel that the foundation of our lives is shaky, not just spiritually, but in other areas too? There will always be "storms" in life, and we must prepare for them.

We need to build a solid financial base to handle emergencies when they come. We should prepare physically by maintaining a strong immune system through healthy habits. And most importantly, we must build a strong spiritual foundation.

Jesus said He came so we could have life and have it more abundantly, but is that possible without a firm spiritual base? In this parable, Jesus teaches that simply hearing His words isn't enough; our actions must align with them.

Years ago, an evangelist came to our church in Ottawa, Kansas. He was an excellent speaker with a lot of good things to say. I had the opportunity to have lunch with him, my dad, and our minister after one of the morning sessions. While we were eating, a young man came up and said he had attended the morning service and wanted to talk to the evangelist. The evangelist brushed him off, saying, "This is not the time or place to talk."

He was right: it wasn't the right time or place, but it was *how* he said it: his tone and attitude. He missed a golden opportunity to make a real impact on that young man's life. He also lost the chance to have any further influence on mine. After that, I didn't pay much attention to what he said. His words and actions didn't match.

As Zig Ziglar said, "People don't care how much you know until they know how much you care."

Building a solid foundation means centering our lives around the life and teachings of Jesus, not just in knowledge, but in our daily actions.

C.A.R.E.

Most personal growth teachings emphasize balancing all areas of life: business/work, home, social, physical, mental, and spiritual. While the spiritual area is the most vital, neglecting the others can have a ripple effect because all are interconnected.

Skip Ross once told a story about being on a speaking tour with a world-famous bodybuilder. During lunch, Skip asked him how long it took to develop his body. The man said it took ten years — working eight to ten hours a day, seven days a week. When Skip asked if it was worth it, the man replied that he would give it all up in a minute to have his family back.

If we don't eat well, exercise, or rest, what happens to our health or mental clarity? Due to the current times, it's easy to get out of balance, both physically and mentally, by not exercising enough or eating poorly. I haven't been exercising as much as I used to, and I can feel the difference in my energy levels. When I'm out of balance physically, it affects me mentally too.

Jesus is still active in our world today, but He works through us. Can He work through us effectively if we aren't centered and balanced? It isn't selfish to take care of ourselves first. Jesus said we must remove the plank from our own eye before helping remove the speck from someone else's. We can't pour from an empty cup.

If Jesus were here with us physically today, what examples would He use to teach the same lessons He taught 2,000 years ago?

A member of our church, Nancy Eure, gave me a great example for this one:

"Yesterday, Eddie and I noticed leaves from our maple tree all over the ground. It hadn't been particularly windy, so we couldn't figure out why so many leaves were falling. When I looked up, I saw the reason: a very young squirrel was gathering leaves and building a nest. I watched as it collected as many leaves as it could fit in its mouth, ran to a fork in the tree, and placed them with others it had already gathered.

Later, when I looked again, our yard was littered with fallen leaves, and there was no sign of that nest. I'm pretty sure the little gusts of wind had blown the squirrel's home away. That young squirrel worked hard, but it hadn't chosen the right materials to build its home."

That reminded me of a song I learned about building a house on sand rather than on solid ground.

When I worked in window treatment design, I sometimes had clients who insisted on using certain materials that didn't drape or hang the way they imagined. They were often disappointed with the result. Choosing the right materials is essential to achieve the outcome you want, whether it's curtains or the foundation of your life.

The Parable of the Good Samaritan

Luke 10:30–37

Today, seek expert advice on all things. Let God guide you and choose to build your life on solid ground.

First, I learned a lot about this road from Jerusalem to Jericho.

Jerusalem is 2,300 feet above sea level, and Jericho is 1,300 feet below sea level. So, in about 17 miles, there's a drop of 3,600 feet. This road, or more like a path, goes through the desert. It's a hazardous route, a happy hunting ground for thieves and robbers. It was called "The Red" or "Bloody Way."

So, let's look at the characters in this parable.

The Traveler

No sensible person would travel this road alone, especially if they had anything valuable. He was reckless and brought a lot of his problems on himself. But haven't we all done foolish things that created problems for ourselves?

The Priest

Why didn't he stop? He may have been traveling from Jericho to the temple in Jerusalem to serve. If he touched a dead body, he would have been considered "unclean" and unable to perform his duties. There were 24 families of priests, and those chosen for duty at the temple were selected by lot; it may have been his only chance to serve in his lifetime. I can understand his reason for not stopping.

But the point is that he chose ceremony above charity. Temple service meant more to him than this man's pain.

The Levite

What was his excuse? Robbers sometimes used a decoy to lure people close enough to ambush them, so he may not have wanted to risk his safety. He might also have been on his way to the temple to assist the priests.

Before we become too critical, how many times have we chosen not to give a hitchhiker a ride or passed a stranded motorist without offering to help? Sometimes, helping could put us or our families in danger.

The Samaritan

In storytelling, there were usually three characters. Jesus' audience would have expected the third to be an Israelite, so His choice of a Samaritan would have shocked them. The Samaritans were the most racially hated group of the day.

When Assyria conquered that area in 722 BC, the Samaritans intermarried and were no longer considered a pure race. They also opposed the rebuilding of the temple in Jerusalem and built their own on Mount Gerizim, believing that it was the true place to worship God.

The Samaritan was the exact opposite of the lawyer. This shattered all stereotypes of who the Jews thought were the people of God. It removed all social, economic, and racial barriers regarding who could be considered a "neighbor."

So, what do we know about the character of the Samaritan?

His credit was good the innkeeper trusted him.

He was more interested in helping than in dogma.

In the end, will we be judged by our creeds or by the lives we live? Our words and actions must align.

Now that we've looked at the characters in this parable and why they didn't help the victim, let's look at the lessons we can learn and how we can apply them to our lives today.

Before doing that, let's consider the lawyer and why he asked Jesus this question. Scripture says he wanted to test Jesus. Was he trying to trap Him, or was he genuinely searching for the truth?

Jesus turned the question back on him. Devout Jews wore small leather boxes on their foreheads, arms, and wrists called *phylacteries.* These contained the scriptures that the lawyer quoted in response to Jesus' question.

Now, let's consider the lessons we can take from this.

Isn't it interesting how Jesus made the lawyer answer his own question? It was hard for him to argue since the answer came from his own mouth. That's a great model to follow when handling disagreements: instead of giving your answer, ask others to share what they think first.

Jesus broke all barriers by choosing a Samaritan to be the hero of this parable. Anyone who needs help is our neighbor, regardless of race, religion, nationality, or even sexual orientation, even if they may have brought their problems on themselves.

We've all done things that didn't turn out well. Nobody needs to remind us; we already know. People don't grow in an atmosphere of criticism. We need to be accepted as we are and helped to learn from our mistakes.

The help we give must be practical. I'm sure the Priest and the Levite felt sorry for the victim—maybe they even said a prayer—but they didn't *do* anything to help.

The people who come to our food pantry don't need to be reminded that they may be there because of poor choices or missed opportunities. They need to be accepted as they are and where they are at this point in their lives. They need food and a word of encouragement.

What Jesus said to the lawyer, He says to all of us: *"Go and do likewise."*

Here's a question for each of us to reflect on: Who do you identify with the most—the Priest, the Levite, the Samaritan, or the Lawyer?

There are times when I see myself in all of them.

Parable of the Rich Fool

Scripture: Luke 12:13–34

Jesus was a master at using something that had just happened, or something someone had said, to teach the principles He wanted to teach.

The custom of this time was to split the inheritance: two-thirds to the older son and one-third to the younger son. If neither son was still living, the inheritance would go to the daughters, but they had to marry within the tribe so the inheritance would stay within the tribe.

It was also customary to take a dispute to a respected Rabbi. Jesus could see that the real challenge was greed and attachment to possessions, which is why He told the parable.

If you look closely at the parable, there is no indication that the farmer got his wealth by cheating anyone or stealing. He didn't mistreat any of his workers. He was a hard worker. He planted his crop and was fortunate enough to have the weather cooperate to allow him to have a great harvest. It's what he decided to do with his abundance, where he failed to measure up.

Here are some observations from *The Interpreter's Bible:*

- **Preoccupation with possessions:** His whole life revolves around himself and his possessions. The parable doesn't say that it's wrong to have wealth; it's about what you do with that wealth and whether you allow it to be the center of your life. This parable exposes the emptiness of a materialistic way of living.

- **Security in self-sufficiency:** He doesn't need anyone else. He thinks he can now sit back and do whatever he wants. Is this what retirement is supposed to be like? There will come a time in all our lives when the only thing that will matter is the relationships we develop with others and with God.

- **The grasp of greed:** The man never even entertained the thought of using the excess to help others. He has no sense of responsibility to anyone else and seems to be ultimately without compassion. I like John Wesley's philosophy: *"Earn all you can, save all you can, and give all you can."*

- **The hollowness of living just for yourself:** This man is describing what most people think retirement should be like. I have to admit, I felt a little like that. Retirement should be when you can do some things you couldn't when working full-time, but that can get old quickly. We all want to feel like our lives have value and matter. Living just for yourself will never give you that feeling of significance.

- **Practical Atheism:** This man lived life as if there was no God. What difference should our faith in God make in the practical matters of life?

Here's a story from The Interpreter's Bible that was meaningful to me:

"A televised interview with a man who had lost his house and all his possessions to a raging brush fire driven by Santa Ana winds in California provides a striking contrast to the rich fool. Recalling that his brother had recently mused that they should be careful not to allow their possessions to possess them, this man, who had just seen everything he owned but the shirt on his back go up in smoke, announced to the reporter with a note of unexpected triumph: 'I am a free man now!'"

Parable of the Fig Tree

Scripture: Luke 13:6-9

The quality of the soil in this area could have been better. It wasn't unusual to see several different kinds of trees in the same vineyard. Because quality soil was so scarce, if something didn't produce, it was removed and replaced with something that would.

It usually takes three years for a fig tree to produce fruit. The gardener convinced the vineyard owner to give it one more year. The gardener said he would dig around it and fertilize it. The gardener wanted to give the fig tree one more chance.

Several vital lessons in this parable can directly impact our lives today. I want to share five of the ones I see, each of which can guide our spiritual growth and self-reflection.

The parable teaches us that the soil of our lives is supposed to produce a yield. We are not here by accident. We have a purpose and the ability to accomplish that purpose. We are part of God's master plans. How does it feel to know that God has included us in His master plans?

We have a responsibility to produce a yield. Uselessness invites disaster. Do you know people who only seem to take from life and never give anything back? Jesus said He came so that we could have life and have it more abundantly. Is it possible to have that abundant life without giving back to society?

Think about some of the happiest times in your life—what were you doing? We will probably find that some of the happiest times were when we were adding value to the lives of someone else.

William Barclay says that we will be judged by the

opportunities we have. Are we preparing ourselves to be able to take advantage of the opportunities when they come our way?

We are supposed to be the gardeners for someone else's fig tree. What we say and do can affect the outcome of someone's life. Judy and I were watching *Finding Your Roots* one week, and Bill Hader, the comedian, was one of the people featured. He is famous for his impersonations on *Saturday Night Live.* When he was in college, he was not sure what he wanted to do. He took a course in comedy, and someone said, "Bill, you're good at this." No one had ever told him he was good at something. It changed the whole direction of his life.

Another guest was Kehinde Wiley. When he was young, he showed an interest in art. His mother sacrificed to ensure he had art supplies and nurtured his interest in any way she could. Today, he is a very famous portrait artist. President Obama chose him to paint his portrait.

We never know how something as simple as a smile or a word of encouragement can affect someone's life. Who are the "fig trees" in our lives that we need to be the gardener for?

Therefore, we need to give others second chances as well. What about us? Do we need to provide ourselves with second chances, too? I think the most complex person to forgive is ourselves. Everyone makes mistakes. The question is, did we learn anything?

Failures and mistakes are our teachers. God's grace is evident in the parable, giving the fig tree a second chance. What happens if we fail to respond to God's second chances? Does God shut us out, or do we shut ourselves out?

Have you ever felt God nudging you in a certain direction? Have you ever not responded to that nudging? What was the result? If it didn't turn out so good, was that God's fault or ours?

If there is something we feel we should do or someone we should reach out to, don't wait. There will eventually be an end, but we don't know when that end will be. Don't wait until you have all the answers before you act. You will never have all the answers.

Remember, God can't steer a parked car. We have to be in motion for there to be any need for God to give us guidance. We will never know what God can do through us unless we try.

The Lost Coin

Scripture: Luke 15:8-10

The parable of the lost coin is one of three parables, one after the other, with the same basic message. The Pharisees and religious rulers of the day were criticizing Jesus for eating with tax collectors and those they considered to be sinners. These parables were in answer to their criticism. The first in this series is the lost sheep, followed by the lost coin, and the last is the prodigal son.

Theologians say that the message is the one unique thing that Jesus taught. Everything else Jesus taught is in other scriptures and writings, and that is that God seeks to save us, to bring us back into a personal relationship with Him. The Jewish people had never conceived of God like that. Their idea of how people could connect with God was by following all the rules they had established. I read somewhere that there were 613 rules plus about 10,000 amendments. Every time a new situation arose that didn't fit one of the 613 rules, they would create a new amendment to cover that new situation. In other words, there was no way anyone could ever have a meaningful relationship with God. So, this picture of God seeking a relationship with us was totally new to them.

In this parable of the lost coin, I asked, "What was the coin, and why was it so important to her?" There are two possible reasons. One was because of its monetary value. It was only worth about 6 cents in today's money, but that was a day's wage in their day. The second reason was sentimental value. The ten coins were worn on a headdress, and it was a sign of a married woman. It would be like our wedding ring today. It was of irreplaceable value to her, just as our relationship with God is of irreplaceable value to us.

The second question I asked was, "Why was it so hard to find?" The houses in those days were small and only had one 18-inch window, so there wasn't much light. All she had was a lantern. Also, the floors were made of dirt, covered with dried reeds pressed onto them. Finding that coin was no small task, and it took a lot of time and effort, just as it takes effort and dedication to seek a relationship with God.

This parable is saying that God values each of us and seeks to have a personal relationship with us. But since we have free will, we can accept or reject the invitation. We have to choose.

I certainly don't have the relationship I want with God, but I am moving in the right direction and improving. Jesus said He came so we could have life and have it more abundantly. The only way to have that "abundant life" is to develop that personal relationship with God by following God's example and centering our lives around Jesus's life and teachings.

Parable of the Prodigal Son

Scripture: Luke 15:11-32

In the 1960s, I went to the United Methodist Men's Congress at Purdue University. One of the speakers was Dr. Lloyd Saatjian, the

District Superintendent of Orange County, California. He gave an interpretation of this parable based on the Middle Eastern culture during the time of Jesus. Knowing the culture and the traditions of the times helps us understand the parable as Jesus spoke it and how His audience heard it. I want to share his interpretation as best I can remember it. He said the meaning is the one unique thing that Jesus taught. Everything else that Jesus taught can be found in other places in the scriptures or other writings. Let's look at this verse by verse.

"There was once a man who had two sons. The younger one said to him, 'Father, give me my share of the property now.' So the man divided his property between his two sons."

This would have shocked Jesus's hearers, because the only way for the son to get his inheritance was for the father to retire or for his father to die. In other words, he was asking his father to drop dead.

"After a few days the younger son sold his part of the property and left home. He went away to a country far away."

The country he went to may have been just a few miles away. The point is that he left his culture and traditions. To do this was to bring shame not only on his family but on the whole city.

He wasted everything on wild living and ended up with the only job available: feeding pigs. That's the worst job possible for a Jew. It meant that he had hit bottom.

Then he came to himself and realized that even the hired servants in his father's house were better off than he was, so he decided to go home and beg his father to make him as one of the hired servants. The slaves in his father's house were like family, but hired servants had no rights at all. So he practiced his speech to ask for forgiveness and to be made as one of his father's day laborers.

C.A.R.E.

When his father saw him from a distance, he ran to greet him. This would have shocked Jesus's hearers. In the Middle East, old men don't run. So why was he running? He was running to save his son. Because he left his culture, he brought shame on his family and the town. According to Jewish law, he was the same as dead, and by returning he would bring shame on the town a second time. According to Jewish law, they had the right to stone him to death. So the father took upon himself the shame of the son. This is the one thing that Jesus taught that Dr. Saatjian says was unique: that God seeks to save us.

The son starts to recite the ritualistic speech asking for forgiveness and to be made as one of his father's hired servants, but the father interrupts him and tells his servants to get the best robe, put shoes on his feet, put a ring on his finger, and kill the fatted calf. "Let's have a feast, for my son was lost but now is found."

If you don't know the customs of the time and the traditions, you will miss the meaning of all this. The best robe was saved for honored guests. Only family members had shoes. The ring was the family power of attorney. What the father was doing was reestablishing his son as a full member of the family with all the rights that went with family membership.

Now the story turns to the older son, who says he was angry and wouldn't go to the feast. So the father left his guests and came out to beg his older son to come in. Dr. Saatjian tells a family story about a time when his father had guests over. After the meal, the male guests went to the parlor, and he asked his older brother to get the cigars for the guests. His brother was 12 years old and was at his father's right hand to help serve the guests, where the older son was supposed to be. His brother gave his father a loaded cigar. When it exploded, his father knew who was responsible, and he reached for his brother, but he ran, and his father left the table and his guests to chase him. To this day, Dr. Saatjian says that when they get together as a family, they laugh about the cigar exploding, but then the conversation turns to the shame his brother caused his father by causing him to leave the table and his guests.

So here, for the second time, Jesus is saying that God the Father is taking upon Himself the shame of the older son and asking him to come to the table, to be at His right hand, to help Him serve His guests.

Again, Dr. Saatjian says this is the one unique thing that Jesus taught: that God actively seeks to save us and bring us back into the proper relationship with God.

Pharisee and the Tax Collector

Scripture: Luke 18:9-14

We all have areas of our lives that are weaker than others, and this parable talks about one of the weaker areas for me: prayer. Leading an adult Bible study has helped me a lot, but I still have a long way to go. What are the characteristics of effective prayer? According to William Barclay, The kind of pride he's talking about here is the kind of pride that says, *"I'm better than you."*

The Pharisee didn't go to pray to God; he went to inform God of how good he was. Gertrude Bahana, author of *The Late Liz*, said she had a problem with people who looked down on people, but then realized she was looking down on people who looked down on people.

William Barclay lists three main characteristics:

1. No one proud can pray.

2. No one who despises people can pray.

3. True prayer comes from setting our lives beside the life of Jesus.

The Pharisee saw himself as better than the tax collector because he not only fasted on Yom Kippur, the highest holy day of the Jewish calendar, but also fasted two days a week: Monday and Thursday. The reason for those days was that those were the busiest marketing days. He would have a bigger audience to see how holy he was.

He reminded me of the young children who jump into the water from the side of the pool and yell, *"Dad, watch me."* Before we get too judgmental, there have been times in all our lives when we've been guilty of this.

When we compare ourselves with Jesus' life, none of us will fully measure up. We all have a lot of growing to do. We can all pray like the tax collector: "Lord, have mercy on me, the sinner."

This parable invites us to consider the stark contrast between the Pharisee and the tax collector and ask ourselves, *"Where do I stand in comparison?"* While we may never reach complete perfection, if we continue to strive to align our lives with the teachings of Jesus, we can undoubtedly make significant progress in our prayer life.

The Rich Man and Lazarus

Scripture: Luke 16:19-31

The Rich Man and Lazarus is the only parable Jesus told that gives the characters names. The name *Lazarus* means "God is my help." The parable is about the attitude of the Pharisees. They wore purple robes and lived a lavish lifestyle. To give you an idea, the robes they wore cost up to $40 in their money. Compare that to the daily wages of working people at that time—4 cents. That's quite a difference.

It helps me understand the whole parable if I can visualize the scene. The rich man was probably eating his meal in his courtyard. Lazarus was dropped off at his gate, waiting for the crumbs that fell from the table. They didn't have silverware then, so they ate with their hands. When they were through, they wiped their hands on pieces of bread and then threw those pieces away. That was what Lazarus was waiting for.

What was the rich man's sin? He didn't mistreat Lazarus. He didn't kick him or have him removed from his gate. His sin was that he didn't even notice him. Lazarus was just part of the landscape. It was as if he never even existed.

Why was that? To understand that, we must understand the feelings and attitudes toward people like Lazarus. The Pharisees felt God favored them and God was punishing people like Lazarus for past sins. To help them would be to interfere with God's punishment.

Reflecting on the rich man's indifference toward people like Lazarus, it's a sobering moment to ask ourselves:

- *In what ways am I similar to the rich man?*

- *Who are the people I might be overlooking?*

- *What is my attitude toward people experiencing homelessness or those living below the poverty line?*

The rich man's sin wasn't doing something wrong but doing nothing at all.

Our church works well in this area, especially with our food pantry. We are limited in what we can do now, but that will eventually change.

Next, I have to ask myself: What would God have me do? In what way can I effectively notice?

The Unjust Steward

Scripture: Luke 16:1-13

The parable of the Unjust Steward is one of the hardest-to-understand parables Jesus ever told. It's in Luke 16:1–13. The question is: *Why would Jesus use a dishonest person to illustrate a principle?* All three of the parties in the parable are questionable when it comes to honesty.

First, let's look at the people in this parable.

The Steward

He had probably been embezzling from the landowner for some time and finally got caught. Another possibility is that he was charging the tenants too much commission.

The Debtors

Why did they agree to reduce their debt to the landowner? Were they cheating him? By agreeing to reduce their debt, they became part of the crime.

The Landowner

He was probably an absentee landowner and rented out part of his land to tenants for a portion of the yield. Why wasn't he surprised at the steward's actions? Why did he praise him for his shrewdness?

William Barclay says there are four lessons for us in this parable.

C.A.R.E.

First lesson — verse 8:

"For the people of this world are more shrewd in dealing with their kind than are the people of the light." As Christians, we would be better off spending as much time on things that improve our relationship with God as we do on worldly things.

Second lesson — verse 9:

"Use worldly wealth to gain friends for yourselves." It's a lesson on how we should handle our possessions. It's not saying we shouldn't enjoy what we give away or that it is wrong to have possessions. It's how we use them that matters. True wealth consists not in what we keep but in what we've gained through honest effort.

Third lesson — verses 10–11:

If we are not trustworthy in using our small possessions and talents to add value to others, how can God trust us to use even more significant things? William Barclay says that a person's way of fulfilling a small task is the best proof of their fitness or unfitness to be trusted with larger tasks.

Fourth lesson — verse 13:

"No one can serve two masters." In Jesus' day, an enslaved person was controlled by his master, who demanded total devotion. Today, we can have more than one job, sometimes two or three, but whatever we find ourselves doing, we should do for God.

Here is a quote from *The Interpreter's Bible*:

"Most of us will not this week christen a ship, write a book, end a war, appoint a cabinet, dine with a queen, convert a nation, or be burned at the stake. More likely, the week will present no more than a chance to give a cup of water, write a note, visit a nursing home, vote for a county commissioner, teach a Sunday school class, share a meal, tell a child a story, go to choir practice, and feed the neighbor's cat."

"Whoever is faithful in a very little thing is also faithful in much."

Whatever talents God has given you, discover them, develop them, and then use them to serve God by helping others.

Forgiving

Scripture: Luke 7:36-50

There are several interesting aspects to this scripture. Going over those aspects and understanding them will help us better understand the parable and what it says to us today.

Question #1: Why did Simon, the Pharisee, invite Jesus to have a meal with him? Was he a fan? Was he trying to catch Jesus saying something that could be used against him later? Or was he the type that just wanted to associate with celebrities? Did this somehow boost his feeling of importance?

Based on what happens later in the story, it seems to me the last suggestion may be closer to the truth. *(More on that later.)*

Question #2: Why was this woman at the meal without being invited?

The houses of wealthy people had an open courtyard and, when the weather permitted, that's where they had their meal. Anyone could come to hear what an important person had to say. When they were in the courtyard, they reclined on their left elbow with their feet extended behind them, making it possible for her to be at Jesus' feet without interrupting the meal.

Question #3: What were the customs of the day pertaining to guests you invite into your home?

There were three things they always did for invited guests:

1. You greeted them with the kiss of peace.

2. Because the roads were dusty, you had a servant wash the dust off their feet and provide a towel to dry them.

3. You provided a fragrant oil to put on them.

Simon provided none of these for Jesus. So what does this tell us about his attitude toward Jesus? It's interesting that Jesus didn't embarrass Simon by calling attention to this at the time.

Question #4: Why was it so offensive to Simon and the people at the meal for her to let her hair down and use it to wipe Jesus' feet?

In Jesus' day, a woman always had her hair up and only let it down in the presence of her husband, never in public. If she did, it could even be punishable by death.

Why did she do it? She was providing Jesus with what Simon should have provided. She wet His feet with her tears, used her hair to dry them because there was no towel provided, and used her own oil to anoint His feet. Jewish women always had an alabaster vial around their necks for personal use.

So, what are the lessons for us in this scripture?

1. Do we need to examine our motives for doing the things we do? Are we doing them to draw attention to ourselves, or to serve other people?

2. Are we aware of our need for forgiveness, like the woman? Or are we too self-sufficient, like Simon, to realize we have a need for forgiveness?

3. Are we prone to judging other people without knowing their story? Why do they do what they do, or think like they do? Many times, the faults we see in others are the same faults we have ourselves.

4. If I were faced with the same kind of decision she was faced with, would I have the courage to do what I thought was the right thing, regardless of what others may think?

These are just a few of the lessons I see in this scripture. What do you see?

The Shepherd and His Sheep

In this parable, Jesus paints a verbal picture of the life and activities of a shepherd that His audience could easily visualize. It's something they saw all the time. But it's not as easy for us because it's not part of our daily life. It helped me understand the parable to find out what the life of a shepherd in Jesus' day was like. Let me share some of what I learned.

What did a day in the life of a shepherd look like? What were the tools of the trade? How were they used?

Scrip: A bag made of animal skin to carry food like bread, dried fruit, olives, cheese.

Sling: Used to protect themselves and the sheep from wild animals and thieves. They could land a stone right in front of a wandering sheep to make it turn back. Now I understand better how David defeated Goliath.

Rod and staff: The rod was about 3 feet long and had nails embedded in it. It was used for defense. The staff had several uses besides being something to lean on. The shepherd could use it to pull a wandering sheep back or lift it out of a ditch. At night, when entering the sheepfold, the shepherd would hold it over each sheep to count it and examine it to see if it was physically okay.

There were two kinds of sheep pens.

(1) The one described in verses 2–3 is an ordinary sheep pen used by many shepherds at the same time. There was a hired gatekeeper who would only open up to the shepherd. Unlike other countries that used sheep for food, sheep were primarily for their wool, so they were with the shepherd for a long time. The shepherd gave them names. They also had a specific call that the sheep recognized, like a clicking sound with the tongue flicking against the teeth or a high-pitched shrill. The sheep would come out from among hundreds of sheep and follow him.

(2) Verse 9 describes another kind of sheep pen. The shepherd would find a canyon with walls on three sides. The shepherds would narrow the remaining outlet by building a wall of stones and thorn branches. The shepherd would leave a small loop opening. The shepherd would lie down across that opening at night, acting as the gate. Nothing could enter without passing the shepherd.

Jesus also said anyone who entered through Him would be able to go in and out and find pasture. This phrase was a common Jewish phrase used to indicate peace and the ability to travel in and out in safety.

How do you relate to this image of Jesus as the door? How does it make you feel?

Jesus said He came so that we could have life and have it more abundantly. What does an "abundant life" look like to you? How would you describe it?

The Shepherd and His Sheep — Life Lessons

Scripture: John 10:1-18

Now, let's look at the lessons it contains and how we can apply those lessons to our lives today.

In verse 7, Jesus said, **"I am the door of the sheep."** What is He saying here?

The Pharisees had 613 rules, plus 10,000 amendments, that you had to follow in order to have any relationship with God. In other words, the average person couldn't have a personal relationship with God. The door was closed for them. Their way was the way of rules and regulations. Jesus' way was the way of love. Jesus was God's example of how we should live in relationships with others, ourselves, and God. Centering your life around the life and teachings of Jesus is the "door" to a personal relationship with God.

In what way, as a church and individuals, are we to be the "door" for other people? Since Jesus is not here physically, we are His hands and feet. So we must ask ourselves: How do we feel we are doing?

Another way we can be "the door" for Jesus is through our attitudes toward other people. Those outside the church are watching us to see if what we do and say match up. Verbally or nonverbally, they are asking: "Do I want to be a part of this?" "Do they have the answers I'm looking for?"

Jesus said, "I came so they could have life and have it more abundantly." What does an abundant life look like? Everyone probably has a different idea, but here are my thoughts:

First of all, it's going through that door and having a personal relationship with Jesus.

Mark Twain said, *"The two most important dates are the day you were born and the day you find out why."*

I believe we are not here by accident. We all have a purpose and are part of God's master plan. And if that's true, God must have also given us the talents and abilities to accomplish that purpose. Finding your purpose, developing your skills, and then finding ways to use those talents to serve God by serving others would be living an abundant life.

That purpose may not be anything spectacular. It may be caring about people and making them feel loved and that their lives matter.

What does it mean to you?

The Wicked Tenants

Scriptures: John 10:1-5,7-18; Matthew 21:33-46; Mark 12:1-9; Luke 20:9-18

I learned a lot while studying this parable, especially about the nature of God. Jesus was teaching in the temple during the last week of His life, and the religious leaders asked Jesus a question: "By what authority do you do these things?" It was a legitimate question because, unlike the synagogue, where anyone could talk, only priests were allowed to teach in the temple.

Jesus answered by telling them this parable.

Unlike other parables, each element has a meaning and reveals much about the nature of God. The absentee landowner is God. The vineyard is Israel. The tenants are the religious leaders. The landowner's son is Jesus.

The absentee landowner (God) provided the tenants with *everything* they needed to be successful and produce a yield, just as God has given us a purpose and all the talents we need to fulfill that purpose. But God also trusts us enough to allow us to accomplish that purpose in our own way, or even exercise the free will not to use those gifts at all.

Just like the landowner was patient with the tenants and gave them multiple opportunities to get it right and honor their agreement, God is patient with us. After the first refusal, I would have lost my patience. But God is a just God, and justice was eventually served.

In the parable, the vineyard was taken away from the tenants and given to someone else. Spiritually, this represents how it passed from Israel and the religious leaders to the Gentiles and to us.

But just like in the parable, we are responsible for producing results. The question now is: Are we doing any better? Are we using the talents God has given us to accomplish His purpose?

Requirements of True Discipleship

Scripture: Luke:14: 25-33

When I first read this scripture, I thought, "I'm not sure I can be the kind of disciple Jesus talks about." There was a lot I didn't understand. I needed clarification, and I had questions.

C.A.R.E.

I remembered a book I read a few years ago called The Questions are the Answers. The book suggested writing concise questions and then searching for answers. I decided to try that with this scripture. Here are some of the questions I came up with:

1. Where was Jesus going when He said this? And why?

a. Jesus had just left Jerusalem because the religious leaders tried to kill Him. Now He was going back again. He knew He was on His way to face the cross.

2. Why was there a large crowd following Him? And why?

a. The crowd followed Him because they believed He was on His way to establish a kingdom. Their concept of the Messiah was that He would drive out the Romans. Jesus was not this kind of Messiah.

3. What was it like to be a disciple in Jesus' day?

a. There would be no visible source of income or profession. They would have to depend on everything being provided for them. They walked everywhere they went. That would be a scary way to live.

4. Why did Jesus ask them to give up everything to be His disciples? Did He mean we had to hate our family and friends?

a. Sometimes, leaders in the Middle East would make outlandish statements to get people's attention.

b. To ask His followers to "hate" their friends and family would be completely out of character for Jesus. If God is love, as Jesus said, then He would never ask us to hate anyone.

c. Choosing to follow Jesus' way of life is number one. Everything else is second best in comparison.

The question is: "Am I ready to commit to being a committed

disciple?" As William Barclay says in his commentary: "Have I counted the cost?" Where is my Jerusalem? And am I willing to commit to going there?

Invitation to a Wedding Banquet

Scripture: Matthew 22:2-14

The standard procedure for inviting guests to a feast was to send the first invitation long before the feast, and then, when everything was ready, send the second (final) invitation.

In this instance, the invited guests were the Jewish nation. They were invited to be God's chosen people and to be God's example to other nations. They accepted God's invitation but didn't follow through. They got caught up in everyday activities. It wasn't that they chose wrong things; it was that they chose second best. The things they chose were not wrong; they just put them ahead of serving God.

So, in the parable, because the Israelites didn't do what they were chosen to do, God didn't change His plans; He just found other people to do what He wanted done. He went to the Gentiles, the Samaritans, the outcasts of the day.

What's the lesson for us here? If my understanding is correct, we are not here by accident. We have been given a purpose by God. We, like the Israelites, can choose to answer that call or not. God won't change His plans; He will just find someone else.

There is one troubling verse in this parable, verse 7, that speaks of the king sending an army. Some theological scholars feel that this verse is out of place. It was not found in the original parable as Jesus told it. When Matthew wrote his gospel (80–90 AD), the Romans were destroying the temple. This was the result of the Jews not accepting

Jesus and following His ways, the way of love.

Master and His Servant

Scripture: Luke 17:7-10

This parable is a shift of focus for Luke. Most parables answer the religious leaders' challenges; now the shift is to the disciples. In this parable, Jesus is talking about the relationship of the master with His servants or slaves.

Slavery in Jesus' day was common. One article I read said that 80% to 90% of people in the Roman Empire were slaves. People could become enslaved in two major ways: they could be taken as spoils of war, or they could sell themselves into slavery, often because of debt. Enslaved people had no rights and could be beaten or even killed. Of course, the Bible suggests that enslaved people should be treated with respect. But they could marry and make money, and sometimes they could earn enough to buy their freedom. Sometimes their owners freed them at age 30. The lifespan then was only about 33 years.

We don't have open slavery in America like they had in Jesus' day, so it's hard to find comparisons. Here are a few thoughts that may qualify:

- Do you know anyone who's a slave to debt? With all the easy credit available, it's easy to go into debt without realizing you're getting in over your head.

- How about cell phones, the internet, or TV? My iPhone tells me how much time I spend on them each week, and it's incredible how much time slips by without realizing it.

- How about the habits we develop? We are creatures of habit, and we can develop either excellent or unproductive ones, since we have free will.

- How about the people we associate with? They say we become like the people we spend time with. Without realizing it, we pick up their habits and attitudes.

But what is it that Jesus expects from us? In this parable, He asks us, as His disciples, to be His servants. But He wants us to be His servants willingly, not like the slaves of His time.

Does that mean we have to give up everything and not enjoy life? I don't think so. We are here for a purpose and have the gifts and abilities to accomplish it. But it's up to us to discover that purpose, develop our talents, and use them to serve others.

It doesn't have to be grandiose things. It can be things we can all do, like giving a smile, looking for the good in people and situations, and doing simple things that add value to others' lives and make them feel they matter and are loved.

Jesus said He came so we could have life and have it more abundantly. I think part of that "abundant life" is realizing we are part of God's ultimate plan. We can never do enough to earn God's favor or surpass what's expected. We can never do enough to earn a reward.

Our greatest joy in life may come from accomplishing what we were created to do, and that may be rewarding enough.

Parable of The Wheat and Tares

Scripture: Matthew 13:24-30

This parable offers many relevant lessons for us today. Judy and I grew up in a farming community in Kansas, and there's nothing more beautiful than a fully headed-out wheat field. But when the wheat is still growing, the field is full of weeds too. If you tried to go into the field and pull out the weeds, you would also damage the wheat, so you let them grow together.

The weeds Jesus refers to here are called tares or darnel. The point is that we can't always tell who the "weeds" and "wheat" are, and it's not our responsibility to judge. Only God sees the whole picture of someone's life. And aren't we all grateful that God doesn't judge us solely on the things we did when we were young?

The parable also reminds us that there will be a judgment someday. Our responsibility is simply to be the wheat, to live as an example for others. In today's world, many things make it harder to remain the wheat, so what can we do to protect ourselves and stay good examples?

Here are a few thoughts:

- Center our lives around the life and teachings of Jesus.

- Be mindful of what we allow into our minds, what we watch, read, and dwell on.

- Surround ourselves with people who share the same core values. One of the benefits of belonging to a church fellowship is the quality of the people we associate with.

- Psychologists tell us we become like the people we admire and spend time with.

- What we consistently put into our minds shapes our actions, and actions repeated often enough become habits.

- Our habits end up guiding our lives, so we must develop good ones.

I acknowledge that I am still on a journey of personal growth, but I am growing. During my time as a member of the Kiwanis Club in Ottawa, Kansas, each of us received a picture of Jesus with a message that stayed with me: "Be part of the solution, not the problem." Although I no longer have that card, the message continues to guide my life. I strive to be the wheat, not the tares, and to keep growing personally and spiritually.

New Cloth on an Old Coat

Scriptures: Matthew 9:16; Mark 2:21; Luke 5:36

New Wine in Old Wineskins

Scriptures: 9:17; Mark 2:22; Luke 5:37-38

The message of these two parables is just as relevant today as when Jesus first shared them. Let me give two personal examples from my own experience that illustrate this.

Our daughter and son-in-law were members of a large church in Cary, NC. We attended the dedication ceremony for their new building. The pastor said that if he and Ken, the music minister, were still doing church the same way in 20 years, they would not be doing their job. He explained that we don't have to change the message, only the way we deliver it. The words we use today and our current communication style may not resonate with young people two decades from now. We have to be willing to adapt and be flexible.

After graduating from pharmacy school, I worked with my dad at our family drugstore. Whenever I wanted to change or try something new, he would say, "No, it won't work. We tried it years ago, and it didn't work." He wasn't interested in doing anything differently. He couldn't let go of the old ways of doing things. The tension created by his inflexibility was the reason Judy and I felt we needed to make the changes we did. In the end, it was the best decision for all of us, including my dad.

As Christians, we must remain flexible and open-minded so that the Spirit of God can work through us. There is no possibility of learning anything new if our minds are closed.

Wise and Foolish Servants

Scriptures: Matthew 24:45-51; Luke 12:42-48

The message of these parables is that whatever power or prestige we have been given, whether political, financial, or otherwise, we are to use it for God, not just for our own benefit. The more we are given, the more is required of us.

If there are things we feel we should do but keep putting off, they become "open loops" in our lives, preventing us from being effective in other areas. The time to do something we know should be done is always when we have the opportunity to do it. The point of this parable is the same as the parable about servants remaining watchful; we never know when our time on earth is over. When that moment comes, we want to be found doing the work God has called us to do. Don't put off until tomorrow what can be done today. As Skip Ross would say, "Do it now." Don't allow those open loops to drain your energy.

God's Standard of Judgement

C.A.R.E.

Scripture: Matthew 25:31-46

Only a very few people have been given the gifts and abilities to do great things or become great successes in any field. But that is not God's standard of judgment. God wants and expects us to develop and use our talents and abilities, but His standard is based on how we treat one another. It is based on using whatever abilities we have to serve others.

If you notice in the parable, everything Jesus asks us to do to help and serve others are simple things that all of us are capable of doing. They don't require unique talents; they are based on our attitudes toward other people.

Remember when the rich young ruler asked Jesus what he needed to do to inherit eternal life? Jesus mentioned only two things: love God with all your heart, mind, and soul, and love your neighbor as yourself. God's standard is not based on personal accomplishments but on our attitude and willingness to serve others in simple ways— and to do so without expecting anything in return. We do these things because they are right.

Isn't it interesting that God never sets us up for failure? He never asks us to do anything we don't have the ability to accomplish.

Two Sons, One Obeys, One Does Not

Scripture: Matthew 21:28-32

This parable was directed toward the chief priests and elders in response to their challenge of Jesus. The Jews claimed to be obedient to God but rejected the gospel and the message of John the Baptist, while the Gentiles, who had refused to obey God, repented and accepted the gospel.

I can relate to this parable. There have been times when I agreed to do something and then found an excuse not to do it. And there have been times when I did something, but with the wrong spirit. God wants us to follow Him, not because we feel we have to, but because we want to. There are times when I go to help with our food pantry because I feel I should, but once I get there and see how it helps the people we serve, my attitude changes.

Persistent Widow and Crooked Judge

Scripture: Luke 18:2-8

Just like the parable of the Friend in Need (Luke 11:5–8), the lesson for us is persistence. God is the only one who can see the whole picture. It may not be that the answer is "no"; it may simply be "not yet." It might be that we are not ready. We may have more to learn before we can receive what we are asking for. If the answer truly is "no," it may be because having that thing would not be the best for us. Our prayers should always end with, "Your will be done."

Jesus is not comparing a crooked judge with God; He is contrasting the two. If even a crooked judge eventually responds because of persistence, how much more will God, who loves us, give us what is best for us?

If, through prayer and meditation, we feel sure that this prayer should be answered, then we can ask God: "What do I need to do, or learn, to be ready?" Then we continue to persist with an open mind and a willingness to change direction if necessary.

Epilogue

When I was in college at the University of Kansas, I had a friend named Gene. His father was Jewish, his mother was Catholic, and he was an atheist. Students who called themselves Christians would go into Gene's room and read the Bible to him: "In the beginning…" Gene would pick up any book, turn it upside down, and pretend to read from it: "In the beginning there was dust." It was a big joke to them, but it made me start thinking about what I believed. I couldn't believe like the students who claimed to be Christians, and I couldn't believe like Gene. So I started reading the Bible. I had been raised in the church, but I still didn't know what I truly believed.

Then, after graduating and starting to work with my dad at our family store, I joined the Kiwanis Club. In their new member packet, they had a business-card-sized picture of Jesus. On it were the words: "I dedicate myself to being part of the solution to the world's problems, not part of the problem." I decided to accept that challenge. I haven't always succeeded, but I have tried, and I am still trying.

I believe that Jesus is God's example of how we are to live our lives in relationship with other people and with God. That example is found in the life and teachings of Jesus. Many of those teachings are found in Jesus' parables.

Whatever your faith, living your life centered on the life and teachings of Jesus is the most fulfilling way to live.

– Gerald Briscoe

About the Author

Gerald Briscoe was born in Ottawa, Kansas, on December 8, 1932. After serving three years in the U.S. Navy, he pursued a degree in pharmacy at the University of Kansas, graduating in 1958. That same year, he married his lifelong companion, Judy Hobbs. Together, they built a life centered on faith, love, and family, raising three children, Cathy, Kara, and Ron, and  today are blessed with seven grandchildren, seven great-grandchildren, and one more on the way.

Gerald spent many fulfilling years as a pharmacist, working alongside his father at Briscoe Drug Store before moving to Virginia Beach, Virginia, where he continued his career at Sentara Leigh Hospital until retiring in 1997.

Now retired, Gerald reflects on a lifetime of service, faith, and gratitude. His writings, including C.A.R.E., are his way of sharing what he's learned about living abundantly through love, grace, and a heart that truly cares.